GW01475226

big cat · lion

Jen Collins is an illustrator from Scotland. She likes to draw the great outdoors, the great indoors, and every day occurrences, no matter how insignificant. *www.jen-collins.com*

Cover art: *Lion* © Jen Collins

Published by teNeues Publishing Company
© teNeues Publishing Company.

teNeues

www.teneues.com